How You Can
Get That Job !

How You Can Get That Job!

Application Forms and Letters Made Easy

REBECCA CORFIELD

KOGAN
PAGE

For MT

First published in 1992
Reprinted 1994, 1995

Apart from any fair dealing for the purposes of research or private study, or criticism or review, as permitted under the Copyright, Designs and Patents Act, 1988, this publication may only be reproduced, stored or transmitted, in any form or by any means, with the prior permission in writing of the publishers, or in the case of reprographic reproduction in accordance with the terms of licences issued by the Copyright Licensing Agency. Enquiries concerning reproduction outside those terms should be sent to the publishers at the undermentioned address:

Kogan Page Limited
120 Pentonville Road
London N1 9JN

© Rebecca Corfield 1992

British Library Cataloguing in Publication Data

A CIP record for this book is available from the British Library.

ISBN 0–7494–0615–1

Typeset by DP Photosetting, Aylesbury, Bucks
Printed and bound in Great Britain by
Clays Ltd, St Ives plc.

Contents

Introduction   7
    The importance of application forms 7
    How to get the most out of this book 7

1. The Process of Applying for Jobs   9
    Why do we have application forms ? 10

2. What are Employers Looking For?   13
    How jobs are advertised 13
    The need to sell yourself 14
    How to approach the task 15

3. What to Put in Your Application   17
    The planning stage 17
    The preparation stage 26

4. Presentation   33
    Spelling 38
    Writing or typing? 38
    Improving your writing 39
    Style 39
    Layout 40
    Additional sheets of paper 40
    Some common problems 41

5. Guidelines and Examples   45
Keeping records 45
Follow-up 45
Examples 46
Dos 53
Don'ts 53

6. Letters of Application   55
Examples 56

7. How to Get That Job!   63
Step-by-step checklist 63
Application form blanks 69

Sources of Help   85

Further Reading from Kogan Page   87

Introduction

The importance of application forms

Do you find that you complete application forms as well as you can, but are not invited to interview? Something about the way in which you make your application must be holding you back.

Applying for jobs is a complicated procedure. It is also a skill that we are never formally taught and we are rarely able to see examples of other people's efforts. Yet the application form or letter that you send in pursuit of a vacancy is the only deciding factor in whether or not you are asked to an interview.

It is vital in a competitive job market to present yourself in the best light. This is not easy but there are ways to improve your techniques so that your application stands out from the rest. All job-seekers can benefit from having well thought-out and presented application forms. In addition to applying for jobs, there are often forms to complete before starting college courses or government schemes.

How to get the most out of this book

This book takes you through the whole process, starting from the beginning when the application form lands on your doormat through to posting the completed document. It establishes a system for job applications which enables you to take more control of the operation. Good candidates are not born lucky; they put time, effort and enthusiasm into the task in order to succeed. This book will be especially useful to the first-time job-seeker who wants to know how to stand a good chance of being selected for interview but, even if you have completed many forms before and are a veteran interviewee, it is easy to become sloppy about your paperwork.

By reading this book, you will be able to check that you are making the most of your skills, experience and personality on every form that you send off. You will come over more effectively to employers and this will enable you to get on more interview shortlists. When you are faced with a blank application form, or need to write a letter applying for work, it can be difficult to know where to start, especially if you are not sure what the employer is really looking for. This book takes you through the various stages and shows you what applying for jobs is all about.

Chapter 1 explains what is involved in the process of applying for jobs. It discusses the application form as one method of finding a job and points out the most important aspects of its completion. Chapter 2 analyses exactly what employers are looking for when they want to take on staff. To improve your chances of success you need to pin-point the most important aspects of the job from the employer's point of view. Spending time thinking about the job on offer and researching the organisation concerned can provide all the answers that you need. In Chapter 3 a typical application form is examined and each section is studied in turn to explain what sort of information should be included. The way that forms look is as important as the information they contain and aspects of presentation are covered in Chapter 4. Chapter 5 runs through examples of difficult or unusual questions together with suggested answers. A list of dos and don'ts for completing forms is included. Chapter 6 shows how letters of application can be written effectively, detailing what to include and how to express yourself. The concluding chapter gives a checklist of steps for approaching the tricky task of filling in job applications and takes you through the steps involved.

CHAPTER 1
The Process of Applying for Jobs

This sort of advertisement appears regularly in newspapers, inviting interested candidates to contact the company if they want to know more about the job on offer.

ADMINISTRATIVE ASSISTANT

Flexible person wanted to help run busy solicitor's office. Clerical experience preferred but training given. Full-time, £12,500 pa.

Application and job description from:

S & J Matthews
Solicitors
150 The Grange
Kelmsworth
Northants

Closing date 20/9/93.

Job advertisement

If, after seeing an advertisement like this, you are interested in applying for the job, contact the employer and ask for an application form and further details. Enclose a stamped addressed envelope for the company to return the application form to you. When you write or phone, if it is not clear from the advertisement, ask if there is a job description available. Make sure that you keep the original details of the advertisement in case you are not sent any additional information.

Why do we have application forms?

It is worth spending a little time analysing exactly what the application procedure is all about. When employers advertise for new staff they know that they will attract a wide variety of candidates. They want to find out about each applicant in order to assess which one will be the most suitable for the job on offer.

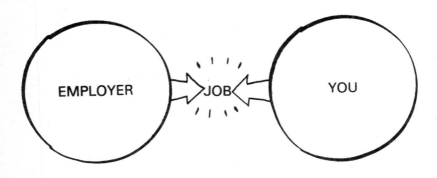

In the first instance, candidates are asked to write to the employer, either by sending in their curriculum vitae (CV) with a covering letter, or by filling in an application form.

Both these approaches will be covered in this book. Application forms are used because employers need some method of comparing the abilities, experience and personalities of those people who apply. A form which asks each person exactly the same questions means that quick comparisons can be made between different candidates.

The types of forms used by employers vary considerably. They can be any length – from one short page to seven or more pages – and they are usually printed. The exact number and types of question depend on the nature and level of the job concerned. Some smaller organisations have one form for every job in the company. This can make it difficult to fill in for jobs that require fuller answers. The questions have been set for every job from Chief Executive to cleaner!

Students are sometimes asked by employers to complete a special type of form called the Standard Application Form. This is a general form which can be used to apply to different companies where candidates are not expected to have much work experience. It contains no printed details of the post applied for or the company where the vacancy exists – these are filled in by the applicant. Copies can be found in student careers offices at colleges. Do not think that this form is taken less seriously because of its name, but to be successful your application must stand out from the crowd.

It is possible to take more control of the application stage of job-hunting. Employers only ask you to complete their forms because they are interested in finding out all about you. However, it is difficult to represent yourself properly when you are relying on just a few sheets of paper. The challenge in applying for jobs is to find ways to make yourself sound interesting enough for the employer to want to invite you for an interview.

Sometimes able and well-qualified candidates are put off applying for suitable jobs because they are daunted by the prospect of filling in a complicated form for a particular job. Pages of questions which require thought and careful preparation can appear confusing and difficult at first reading. It is unusual to find a new job without having to fill in some kind of paperwork, so the more forms you complete, the better your chances of success – as long as you do it well.

Making applications for jobs is a serious matter. Each one needs time and care in order to complete it properly. However, even the most difficult form can be tackled successfully given the proper technique. It makes sense to establish a system to ensure that you give yourself every possible chance to get the job of your choice. As with any difficult task, splitting the work up into smaller less daunting parts can be helpful. Application forms lend themselves well to this approach. The next few chapters explain in detail how to organise yourself to be successful. In addition to using good techniques, you need to be in the right frame of mind to 'sell yourself' effectively on paper. To establish yourself in the mind of the employer as someone worth interviewing, you must believe it yourself!

The only way to get a job is to keep making applications to different employers. Assuming that you fill in your forms to a high standard and are applying for suitable jobs, you are bound to succeed eventually. Applying for a series of jobs at the same time not only increases your chances of success but also ensures that you do not build up your hopes of any one job in particular. You will not be so disappointed at rejection for a certain position if you know that you have other applications in the pipe-line, any of which could be successful.

CHAPTER 2
What Are Employers Looking For?

How jobs are advertised

Jobs can be advertised in a variety of ways. One of the most common ways of hearing about vacancies is through newspapers, although other methods involve advertisements in local shops; word of mouth; local radio stations; and professional or specialist journals. Certain local and national newspapers carry advertisements for jobs in every issue, often with different types of work being advertised on different days. The interested job-seeker is asked to apply in writing with a CV or send off for an application form. Companies will often send out information about their products or services, as well as a description of the job vacancy concerned.

However, many jobs are never advertised at all. Research suggests that approximately 70 per cent of all jobs are filled without being advertised. Sometimes employers wait for potential applicants to contact them. Chapter 6 tells you more about the way to write impressive letters of application to send with your CV or ask employers if they have vacancies. Some employers tell their existing staff that there is a vacancy and invite applications by word of mouth.

Application forms are one method of giving an employer information about your suitability as a candidate for a particular post. An example is shown on page 70. The form may be any length but is usually between two and four pages. Normally printed in black ink on white paper, it contains a series of questions designed to encourage the applicant to give certain information about him or herself.

The need to 'sell yourself'

Application forms need to contain positive statements about yourself. It is not enough to give a list of what you have done and the skills that you have acquired. You need to see application forms principally as a method for you to 'sell yourself' to an employer. In today's competitive job market, there will be many hopeful applicants for every job. Only the most distinctive application forms will stand out enough for the senders to be picked for interview.

It used to be true that anyone who could satisfy the minimum conditions laid down in a job description would automatically be shortlisted for interview. Although it is true to say that applicants will not be picked for interview without establishing that they fulfil the basic conditions, because of the increasing number of candidates it is now essential to put forward a much stronger application. This means convincing the employer that there would be some extra benefit or added value in including you in the shortlist for interview. More applicants mean that the criteria for each job are raised and employers can afford to be more choosy. In other words, you have to try harder in order to succeed.

Companies are looking for the best candidates for their vacancies and your application needs to shout out loud that you are that candidate. But judgement about who is the best candidate will vary according to the job on offer. That is why it is essential to get inside the head of the employer to examine what exactly he or she is looking for with each vacancy. One way to impress people is to show enthusiasm. You are in competition with many other keen applicants who are all trying to impress. A genuine interest and excitement about the work involved in the job show even through the written page.

Consider the following two examples in answer to the question:

'Why do you think that you are suitable for this position?' (working as an accounts assistant)

John's answer: 'I am quite good with numbers. My last job involved calculating and checking figures and I tried to be accurate. I took GCSEs in mathematics and did well at school in this subject.'

Michelle's answer: 'Working with numbers is a challenge. I take a great pride in being accurate and did especially well in the mathematics GCSE course at school. I very much enjoyed my last job which involved a great deal of figure work, calculating totals and checking figures for the department I worked in. I am keen to make my career in this area.'

You can see how Michelle's reply abounds with energy and enthusiasm for the work. She creates the feeling that she would come in to work each Monday morning beaming with delight at the prospect of a new week!

How to approach the task

Application forms are split up into different sections and each is concerned with a different subject. Their sole purpose is to find out about the candidates and those candidates whose forms contain the most impressive information will be invited for interview. However, it is extremely difficult to put yourself across effectively on paper alone. To create a good impression you need to give the employer as *full details* as possible about yourself. Applicants who do not write much are doing themselves out of their best chance of getting the job.

The most important point to remember is that *neatness* gives you a great advantage in the hunt for the job of your choice. It has been shown that employers will reject perfectly well-qualified, suitable candidates if they send in badly presented applications. There are two reasons for this. The first is that how a document looks creates a strong first impression. The only information that the employer has to go on to decide whether to pick you for interview is your application form. He or she will make judgements about your attitude to work and other people on the strength of the way you have filled in your form. The second reason is that it is hard to take in information from the printed page, let alone the hand-written one, and neat writing is much easier to follow than messy scrawl. Your application forms need to be as well presented as possible to stand out from the rest without being distracting.

Sometimes it is tempting to send in your CV instead of spending time filling in the same information on the form. However, if the employer wanted your CV, he or she would have asked for it. To send it as a substitute for filling in an application form tells the employer that you cannot really be bothered to spend time applying for the job. It also shows that you are not prepared to follow instructions. Of course, if the company asks to see your CV in addition to your application form that is quite a different matter. In this case the CV should be short and concise. More than two or three pages will be too long to hold the reader's interest. But when you are answering the questions on the application form you need to make your answers long enough to interest the employer without being long-winded.

The well-written response that drags on is liable to bore the reader just as much as the poorly written one. To make sure that your answers are written in a coherent way, you must *organise* your thoughts in advance. Chapter 3 gives more information about thinking through and planning your answers systematically before you start to write anything. This ensures that you do not duplicate, muddle up or miss out any information.

CHAPTER 3

What to Put in Your Application

The secret of filling in application forms is to take the task seriously. If you are not prepared to devote a certain amount of time to this activity, you are probably not serious about the job itself. Getting the job you want is a serious business and demands the same care and time that you would devote to a college essay or a school project.

If you are not keen enough to allow sufficient time for completing the form, the employer will realise this and you will not get the job. My rule of thumb is that you should aim to spend at least one day of preparation for each page of the application form. Of course, not all sections of the form will take as long as each other, and you will not be spending the whole of each day poring over pieces of paper, but this is a rough guide to how much input each job application requires. You may feel that this is a lot of exertion for each job, but think about what you have to gain. The salary (or wages) that you would earn in a year amounts to a lot of money, and is surely worth the investment of some effort. The best way to approach filling in the form is to split the task up into easy stages.

The planning stage

The task
When the application form arrives on your doormat, take a photocopy of it. Libraries, job clubs and local shops often have photocopying equipment, although you may have to pay for your copies. If you do not have access to a photocopier, write out the

questions by hand on to scrap paper, then put the original form away for safe keeping. You will now only be working on the copy that you have made until you are confident that you have sorted out exactly what to say for each of your answers.

The secret of a good application is to allow yourself plenty of time before the closing date – preferably a day for each page of the form. Impressive writing cannot be done when you are feeling pressurised and rushed. Find a quiet place where you can concentrate on the task in hand. You will need a clear desk or table with enough space to spread out all the relevant pieces of paper and a good light by which to read and write. Try to make sure that you will not be disturbed, and switch the television off! Now is the time to concentrate on this task alone, in order to immerse yourself in all the details of the job. Have a current copy of your CV to hand to give you the facts and dates about your career history. Your favourite type of music played quietly in the background may help to put you in the right mood.

The vacancy
Before you start, re-read the details of the job carefully. Take a note or underline the main requirements/skills/qualifications asked for. If you do not have any of these requirements it is unlikely that you will be asked to an interview. However, if you do have skills and experience or alternative qualifications to those specified and feel that you could do the job, go ahead and apply. Many people get good jobs by taking chances like this, on the basis that they do not have anything to lose. However, the onus is on you to state clearly what you *are* offering as an alternative to the qualifications or experience asked for and why your background makes you suitable for the position.

A certain amount of time must be spent thinking through the nature of the vacancy for which you are applying. Each job is different and requires different qualities, skills and experience. Moreover, every organisation has a different feeling or culture and is looking for people who will fit in. The big, bustling, high-street department store will be looking for candidates who can work happily in that environment, while the small country firm of solicitors will require a different type of staff.

Yourself

At the planning stage you also need to spend time thinking in some depth about who you are and what you have to offer relative to the company and its requirements. You should prepare a good CV which gives details about your qualifications and experience to date. This can be used as an *aide-mémoire*, or memory-jogger, to fill in certain parts of your application form and also as a confidence booster at a time when you need to be thinking about your achievements. A properly written CV can give an overview of your strengths and skills and help you to present yourself well when applying for jobs. It is vital to link your skills, knowledge and experience to the duties involved in the job.

Now is the time to inflate your own self-confidence as much as possible. On most application forms there is a question about your personal qualities and how these will enable you to contribute to the post on offer. Most of us could reel off a long list of our faults but we find our strengths more difficult to pin-point. For this exercise, you will need to dispense with the feeling that you are boasting, take a deep breath and describe yourself in the best possible light.

Exercise: Your good points

Most people find this exercise tricky because we are not used to applauding ourselves in this way, which is exactly why it is such a useful thing to do. Perhaps you can remember being complimented on some facet of your character or behaviour, either in person or in a school or college report. You may have had favourable comments made about you in an appraisal from a previous workplace. What was said then? How would your best friend describe your good points to someone who had not met you before?

In the space overleaf make a list of ten of your good qualities. Each point should comprise one word or short phrase and relate to your behaviour. Here are some examples. You may find some which apply to you and could be included in your list:

flexible
calm
punctual
sensible
quick to learn
practical
polite
lively
dedicated
creative
confident
approachable
assertive
accurate
perceptive
consistent
innovative
careful
strong
direct
adaptable
bright
thoughtful
imaginative
dependable
friendly
outgoing
serious-minded
quick

articulate
organised
tactful
alert
reliable
cooperative
loyal
responsible
versatile
good at keeping to deadlines
able to work under pressure
hardworking
capable
thorough
able to work alone
good team member
committed
good at managing others
competent
humorous
decisive
enthusiastic
cautious
patient
dynamic
methodical
self-motivated
sensitive

Everybody's list will be different according to the personality of the writer. Write your description here:

1

2

3

4

5

6

7

8

9

10

This type of list is useful for two reasons. First, it provides you with the raw material to answer questions about your strengths or personal qualities and second, it enables you to see your good points laid out on paper as a boost to your confidence. If you are an appropriate candidate for a job vacancy, you of all people need to feel confident that you have the personality and experience to do the job well. Unless you believe it, you will not be able to convey that impression to anyone who reads your application form. So spend some time thinking about yourself, what you have been praised for in the past and the advantages to an employer in taking you on.

Your experience
You also need to plan which aspects of your past to mention. Large gaps in your career history will be noticed, but this still leaves you with a certain amount of leeway as to how you tell the story of your experience to date. Generally, information provided by you must be relevant to the job (and so will change with the different jobs that you apply for) and should have purpose. Otherwise, the good points that you include will be lost in general trivia that do not add anything to your form. The way that information is put over has an impact on the way it is received. It will never be relevant to divulge that you failed a flute exam at school, but it may be worth saying that you studied the instrument when you were younger.

Active verbs or power words can be useful in describing your achievements to date. The following list may prove helpful when you are writing about your experience. There are many other words which may apply to you but here are some examples:

coordinating	inputting
computing	growing
caring	advising
persuading	recruiting
establishing	performing
serving	leading
travelling	developing
diagnosing	filing
assessing	sorting
analysing	typing
copying	loading
negotiating	handling
managing	communicating
training	researching
teaching	selling
memorising	inventing
deciding	recording
checking	stocking
compiling	delivering
carrying	playing
helping	working
mending	making
problem-solving	monitoring
evaluating	interpreting
writing	selecting
reading	translating
cleaning	supervising
driving	planning
drawing	enabling
washing	

If you are applying for a certain type of work, the organisation concerned will want to see evidence of your experience in this field.

A national organisation which recruits volunteers to work abroad always asks candidates if they have done any voluntary work before. Applicants often answer 'No' when it should be obvious that this will not be sufficient. In such a case the employer needs to be convinced that you are capable of sustaining an interest in volunteering. Even if the experience was some time ago it is worth mentioning. Candidates for this type of vacancy with no voluntary experience should join a scheme and get it immediately so that they can fill in the form adequately.

Analysing the job

Deciding what skills and abilities are required is not a matter of guesswork but of using common sense. Consider the following job advertisement:

TREETOPS NURSERY

Small estate-based nursery needs a part-time childcare assistant to help with general duties. 17.5 hours per week. Personality more important than experience. Training given.

For application form write to:

Treetops Nursery, Garrick Estate,
Tonbridge, Kent or phone 000-0000.

Even with these few details we can work out what sort of person would be suitable for the job. We know that the employer is interested in three main things: experience, skills and personality. Let us consider each of these in turn.

Experience
Although the advertisement says that training will be given and experience is not necessary, many applicants will be able to provide some experience so it would be helpful to offer some evidence of your ability to do this type of work. Perhaps you have brought up children of your own, helped out in other childcare schemes or been a babysitter or a childminder in the past. Even

What the employer is looking for

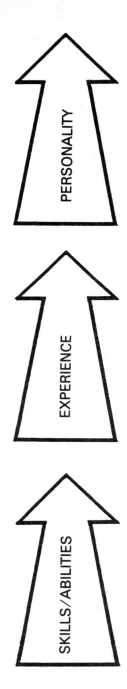

PERSONALITY

EXPERIENCE

SKILLS/ABILITIES

though none of these examples would be classed as 'proper' jobs, they indicate your ability in this area.

Skills
In this sort of work the right person will be punctual and good at time management. Budgeting and organising skills will come in handy as well as attention to detail and the ability to schedule events. Knowledge of home economics would be an asset. An awareness of health and safety is important when working with young children and even confidence with shopping would be a selling point.

Personality
In terms of personality, we have to think about the sort of person who can work with children. He or she needs to be well balanced, reliable and organised, with a tolerant and happy disposition. Someone who is observant and patient, who enjoys playing with and entertaining children of all ages and has an understanding of the problems and concerns affecting children would be ideal. The right person should enjoy teaching and communicating with other people and using his or her imagination. A good childcare worker finds it easy to care for children and is able to create a disciplined environment with the right mixture of fun and control.

These points are the basic requirements for anybody who wants to work with children. To apply for this job, an applicant needs to show that he or she has had this type of experience, together with the skills and personality by quoting examples from previous jobs. Any job can be analysed in this way, even with little information to start with. You need to use your imagination, your common sense and research into what is involved in the job.

Finding out more
If you are not sure what the company is looking for, you need to do some detective work. Research into the products or services sold, the numbers of offices or outlets and staff, the main markets and the style of the organisation is never wasted. It

enables you to feel confident about your knowledge of the business, and you can impress the interviewer by talking up in the interview about your research on the company.

You can try to talk to people who work at the firm by ringing up and asking for information; you can look up facts about different organisations in libraries or ask people who work in similar jobs for their impressions of the company or the type of work that you are interested in.

The preparation stage

Taking care

First, read carefully through the copy that you have made of your form. Then work your way through it considering how you are going to approach filling it in. If you do not read through a form thoroughly before you start to complete it, you can often make unnecessary mistakes. Some forms have duplicate questions that mean you may only need to complete half the form depending on your situation. If you rush to start writing, you may find that you have filled in a section that does not apply to you.

That sort of error can leave you looking at a messed-up form, and feeling demoralised when you badly need more confidence, not less. Sometimes there will be similar sounding questions which require quite different answers, and it is worth checking what the form is looking for in each answer. If you are not totally confident about your spelling, make sure you use a dictionary. There is no excuse for misspelled words. Use ink or ball-point pen and not pencils, crayons or felt-tipped pens. Normally, you need to make your answers fit the space provided, and fill up that space completely. However, if the form suggests that you may like to continue on a separate sheet of paper if you do not have enough room for your answer, you should do so. The employer is saying that he or she expects a longer answer than there is room for on the page. Everybody else who applies for the job will use an extra sheet and, to do your answer justice, you need to do the same.

Completing the different sections

The following sections usually appear on every application form.

Personal details

The first section of the form is concerned with your personal details. These questions ask your name, address and other facts. You will not have any opportunity to 'sell yourself' here. You will normally be asked to give your first and second names in full and your full address. You must give your telephone numbers for home and work (if applicable).

If you are not on the telephone you should find a friend or relative who can take messages for you, should the employer decide to phone you. Make sure that you ask permission before giving out anybody else's number and do not give your current work number if it will cause trouble should a potential employer decide to ring you up.

You will be asked for your date of birth, and sometimes your age as well. You will have to state your nationality and sometimes answer further questions about your eligibility to work in this country. You may be asked for a description of your general state of health. An application for a Civil Service position may ask many more detailed questions about your background, including details about your parents, whether you have ever had any other nationality, your place of birth and so on.

You may be asked where you saw the advertisement for the post. This is to tell the employer how effective the company's recruitment advertising is. It is helpful if you can give precise details.

Academic qualifications

You need to give the names and addresses of places where you have studied. The employer will want to know particulars of qualifications obtained (classes, divisions, etc) and the names of courses or subjects studied, if appropriate. If you have recently left school or college you will be expected to make more of this experience by giving full information about subjects taken or projects worked on.

Work experience

This section of the form is where you expand on your previous work experience. The aim is not just to produce a list of all the jobs that you have ever had, but rather to explain what skills and abilities you have to offer a new employer. Most space on the form will normally be allocated to your current or last job. This is on the understanding that the most recent job will probably be the one which afforded you most responsibility. You will often be asked for a brief outline of the duties performed, and sometimes the salary or wage that you were paid. If you are employed at present you may be asked for details of the notice that you are required to give.

Most forms ask that previous jobs should be put in a logical order (usually, the most recent first) and you will be asked to give details of the posts held, the names and addresses of the employers, and the dates concerned. Sometimes you will be asked why you left each job and the salary at that time. In this case it is important that you give only *positive* reasons for leaving previous jobs. If you complain about former companies, colleagues or employers it will look as if you are a difficult person who is capable of running down the recruiting company in the future.

There may be sections where you are asked to outline your leisure interests and activities. You will need to show that you are a well-rounded person with a variety of hobbies or interests outside work. It helps to have some sporting or active interests and others which use your mind or involve creativity. A selection of different types of activities will show this and as many as eight pastimes could be mentioned. It does not matter if you have not done all the things on your list recently, as long as you would be happy to discuss them in an interview. This means that you must know about or be interested in every item that you write down here.

Equal opportunities

You will sometimes find a question about equal opportunities for jobs with large corporations, voluntary organisations, local authorities or charities. Any organisation which works with the general public may be interested in your attitude to the issues raised by this subject. If you find a question such as 'What does equal opportunities mean to you?' on a form, it requires some thought. Like most difficult questions, there is no precise, correct answer, but the employer will want to know that you take the subject seriously. You need to illustrate this in your response by defining the phrase and saying how it is important to the job. One of the best ways is by using other words to explain it. You could say: 'Equal opportunities mean everyone getting the same chances in employment and access to services.'

In some cases the employer will go further and ask: 'How would you put equal opportunities into practice in this job?' Your answer should contain references to the way that the services in question need to be accessible to all the people being served and what measures could be taken for ensuring that this happens. Treating people fairly applies to staff as well as clients, though, and you should also mention that you are keen to play your part as a sympathetic and supportive team member.

Statement by candidate

This section can appear in various guises. A typical form of words is: 'Give any other information which you consider will be helpful in support of your application.' This will normally be the biggest blank space on the form; it is the section generally left to last and it will require the most work.

The answer that you give should tell the employer what you think you can contribute to the organisation, not why you want to work there. So you must find ways of stressing what you have to offer. Each candidate will be anxious to get the job because of the benefits that come with it, such as the wages, job security etc. What the employer wants to hear is how *you* can add to the work being done by the organisation. Chapter 5 provides guidelines and examples of how to answer such questions.

You need to present your strong points which match the job requirements. From studying the advertisement and information provided about the job, you should be able to highlight these requirements and ensure that, as far as possible, you satisfy them. Remember that you can describe your work experience in different ways. For example, in one case you may emphasise the

29

experience you obtained in handling people and achieving things. In another case, you may need to emphasise the amount of work you did, analysing and interpreting data, preparing reports and contributing to the development of new ideas, policies and procedures. Detail about the precise way in which you worked is not required. What is relevant to the employer are the transferable skills involved in each case.

Employers are interested in three main areas:

- your skills
- your experience
- your personality

You may be asked about your career ambitions. You should convey enthusiasm about the job and imply that you will want to progress within the company without seeming to have way-out or aggressive ambitions.

Referees

You may be asked for particulars of two (or sometimes three) people to whom reference may be made about your suitability for the work concerned and your character. These references are not normally taken up unless you are picked for the job, but you must always ask permission before you put anyone's name down as a referee. You will need a name, title, address and telephone number for each person.

Mind the gap!

We all have aspects of our history which need some explaining. It may involve a time when you were not working for some reason, or a job which ended more abruptly than you would have liked. Whether it is a period of unemployment, some time in prison or detention, or being sacked from a position, you will need to explain, in the most positive way, what happened to you during that time.

Monitoring form

Some employers will send you another form to complete with

your application form. It asks for details of your ethnic origin and if you have any disabilities. Often the form will explain what it will be used for: 'The information contained in this form will help us to monitor the percentage of applicants that we employ from different ethnic groups. On receipt of your application it is filed separately and will not be considered in conjunction with your application.' Sometimes applicants worry that this information may prejudice the employer against them, but this is not the case. The employer is just trying to find out how fair their recruitment policies are and the information will help them to put their equal opportunities policies into practice.

Acknowledgement card
You may find a card has been enclosed with your application form. This is for you to complete with your name and address so that the employer can send it to you when he or she receives your application. Normally, only large companies are this well organised, so return it to them with your application. You will know that your form has arrived safely when the card is posted back to you.

CHAPTER 4
Presentation

The way in which you complete your form is regarded by employers as important. The vital lesson to learn from this book is: *the way that your form looks is as crucial as what you have written on it.* When your application lands on an employer's desk, he or she will give it a three-second glance to gain a first impression before deciding whether it is worth studying more closely. The most comprehensive and well thought-out forms can be ruined because of lack of time and trouble taken in filling them in. No matter how good a candidate you are in theory, if your form does not look neat and easy to ready, you are unlikely to be considered for the job.

To illustrate the importance of this point, study the two examples overleaf. They are simple application forms which contain the same information but are very different in appearance.

I have seen many untidy and messy forms like Janet's which have been carelessly completed with too little time dedicated to the task. Some employers would simply discard her form without even reading it. It is difficult to tell which way she has answered some of the questions and, because she did not draft the form in rough first, her spacing is haphazard and the form is difficult to read.

No doubt Janet thought that companies would be so interested in the content of her form that the way it looked was less important than what it contained. Unfortunately, as you can see, bad presentation, however nice the writing, makes it a trial to read, particularly when there is a pile of 50 other forms to be read.

APPLICATION FORM

Confidential	*(please use black ink)*	When completed, return to:

Application for appointment of: *Technical Assistant* Ref: *EB/C24J*

SURNAME *STACEY*   OTHER NAMES *Janet*
(IN BLOCK LETTERS) Mr /~~Mrs~~/ Miss   *(IN BLOCK LETTERS)*

Maiden name ——— Marital status *Single* Ages of children, if any ———
(if appropriate)

Address *23 Bryan House Rotherhithe Street, London SE16 1HB*

Telephone No. *071-000-0000*

Age *33 yrs.*   Date of Birth *15.4.59*

Are you a registered disabled person? YES/~~NO~~ if yes, state Reg. No. and nature of disability

---

EDUCATION, TRAINING AND QUALIFICATIONS

Schools, Colleges and Universities attended since age 11 *(with dates)*	Qualifications and Certificates obtained *(give dates, grades, subjects)*
Camp Hill School Kings Heath BIRMINGHAM B14 1971 to 1977	*O'Levels — 9 subjects including ENGLISH LITERATURE & MATHEMATICS ALL JUNE 1975 A' LEVELS — ECONOMICS GRADE B, ENGLISH GRADE E. BOTH JUNE 1977*
KINGSTON POLYTECHNIC KINGSTON-UPON-THAMES, SURREY 1977 to 1980	*BA (HONOURS) SOCIAL SCIENCE specialising in Development Studies. Class II June 1980*

Where did you see the post for which you are applying advertised? *EVENING GAZETTE* P.T.O.

PREVIOUS APPOINTMENTS TO DATE

(the most recent first)

Employer's name and address *(and nature of business)*	From	To	Position held and duties	Reason for leaving
Trusty Insurance Co Unit 7 The Park Twickenham Surrey TW9 OPZ (Insurance Company)	1989	Date	Administrative Assistant Filing, answering the phone, writing and posting letters, dealing with the public and keeping the diary. Taking minutes of meetings	I would like to work for the civil service to help the public
Laugdale Motor Company Bernardsey Road Landon SE19 TG	1981	1989	General hand Keeping the office area tidy and answering the phone. Generally helping out by taking messages etc	Offered a position with more variety in an office environment.
Different restaurants (Temporary work)	1980	1981	Various catering jobs in London	To go to a permanent position

NAMES AND ADDRESSES OF TWO REFEREES

(Please give your last employer as a reference if possible)

(1) Ms Deb McKenna (owner) Trusty Insurance Co Unit 7 The Park Twickenham Surrey TW9 OPZ

(2) Mr B Neate (Accountant) 407 The Glades Suffolk Road Mitcham Bedfordshire BD3 1LL

May your referees be contacted for a reference if you are selected for interview? YES/NO

Supplementary questions for posts involving driving or use of a vehicle.

Do you hold a current driving licence? YES/NO If so for what types of vehicle?

Do you own or have the use of a vehicle? YES/NO If so what type?

Signature _Janet Stacey_ Date _3rd May '93_

APPLICATION FORM

Confidential   (please use black ink)   When completed, return to:

Application for ADMINISTRATIVE   Ref: OB/C24J
appointment of: ASSISTANT

SURNAME __STACEY__   OTHER NAMES __CECILIA__
(IN BLOCK LETTERS) Mr/Mrs/Miss   (IN BLOCK LETTERS)
Maiden name __N/A__   Marital status __SINGLE__   Ages of children, if any __N/A__
(if appropriate)
Address __23 BRYAN HOUSE, ROTHERHITHE STREET,__
__LONDON. SE16 1HB.__

Telephone No. __071-000-0000__
Age __33 YEARS__   Date of Birth __15.4.59__

Are you a registered disabled person? YES/NO   if yes, state Reg. No. and nature of disability
__N/A__

EDUCATION, TRAINING AND QUALIFICATIONS

Schools, Colleges and Universities attended since age 11 (with dates)	Qualifications and Certificates obtained (give dates, grades, subjects)
CAMP HILL SCHOOL KINGS HEATH BIRMINGHAM B14 1971 TO 1977	O' LEVELS: 9 SUBJECTS INCLUDING ENGLISH LITERATURE AND MATHEMATICS. ALL JUNE 1975 A' LEVELS: ECONOMICS GRADE B ⎫ JUNE 1977 ENGLISH GRADE E ⎭
KINGSTON POLYTECHNIC KINGSTON-UPON-THAMES SURREY 1977 TO 1980	B.A. (HONOURS) SOCIAL SCIENCE SPECIALISING IN DEVELOPMENT STUDIES. CLASS II. JUNE 1980

Where did you see the post for which you are applying advertised? EVENING GAZETTE P.T.O.

PREVIOUS APPOINTMENTS TO DATE
(the most recent first)

Employer's name and address *(and nature of business)*	From	To	Position held and duties	Reason for leaving
TRUSTY INSURANCE COMPANY. UNIT 7, THE PARK TWICKENHAM SURREY TW9 OPZ (INSURANCE COMPANY)	1989	DATE	ADMINISTRATIVE ASSISTANT: FILING, ANSWERING THE 'PHONE, WRITING AND POSTING LETTERS DEALING WITH THE PUBLIC AND KEEPING THE DIARY, TAKING MINUTES OF MEETINGS.	I WOULD LIKE TO WORK FOR THE CIVIL SERVICE TO HELP THE PUBLIC.
LANGDALE MOTOR COMPANY BERMONDSEY ROAD LONDON SE1 9TG	1981	1989	GENERAL HAND: KEEPING THE OFFICE AREA TIDY AND ANSWERING THE 'PHONE. GENERALLY HELPING OUT BY TAKING MESSAGES ETC.	OFFERED A POSITION WITH MORE VARIETY IN AN OFFICE ENVIRONMENT.
DIFFERENT RESTAURANTS (TEMPORARY WORK)	1980	1981	VARIOUS CATERING JOBS IN LONDON	TO GO TO A PERMANENT POSITION.

NAMES AND ADDRESSES OF TWO REFEREES
(Please give your last employer as a reference if possible)

(1) MS D. MCKENNA
(OWNER)
TRUSTY INSURANCE CO.
UNIT 7, THE PARK
TWICKENHAM
SURREY TW9 OPZ.

(2) MR B. NEATE
(ACCOUNTANT)
407 THE GLADES
SUFFOLK ROAD
MITCHLEY
BEDFORDSHIRE BD3 1LL

May your referees be contacted for a reference if you are selected for interview? YES/~~NO~~

Supplementary questions for posts involving driving or use of a vehicle.

Do you hold a current driving licence? ~~YES~~/NO If so for what types of vehicle?

Do you own or have the use of a vehicle? ~~YES~~/NO If so what type?

Signature *Cecilia Stacey.* Date 3rd May'93

If there was a choice to be made between Janet and Cecilia, which would you pick?

Be aware that particular jobs mean that employers may look for different signs of your potential from your application. With any job concerned with administration, writing or paperwork of any kind the employer will be ruthless about the way that your answers are written. When I recruit people to work with job-seekers, I expect all the applicants to submit beautifully prepared CVs. Similarly, employers offering work concerned with art and design matters will notice the details of your presentation. You should pay particular attention to the way that you space and lay out your writing for this type of work.

The key to a well-presented document is planning and preparation. Although it takes time, you should never write up an application form straight away without composing a rough draft first. This means that you can make your mistakes on the rough version and, when you are happy with your answers, copy them on to your neat, final version. Use lined paper under the final version so that you can keep the lines straight and always use a ruler to underline, end a section or delete information. If you do make an error, cross it through neatly with a single line or use correction fluid to make an invisible repair. Little details like this can mean the difference between success and failure.

Spelling

Bad spelling is inexcusable on application forms and will normally mean that your application will not be read right through, even if it is for a job that does not require a great deal of written expertise. If you know that your spelling and grammatical skills are weak, make sure that you check all the difficult words by using a dictionary and allow extra time to get a good speller to check the form thoroughly for you.

Writing or typing?

Unless you are a skilled typist, it is best to hand-write your form. Application forms are difficult to type because of the need to fit your answers into the spaces provided. Unless you are an expert at the fiddly job of lining up type and calculating how much room your answer will take, your efforts at typing will look much messier than a neatly written form. If you do decide to type or word-process the application, complete one version in rough first to make sure that you have calculated the spacing correctly. Words running off the page, uneven lines and cramped sentences will detract from your answers.

Improving your writing

If you know that your handwriting is untidy, you must allow extra time for this part of the process. Most writing can be improved by using capital (or upper case) letters all the way through the form. It is difficult to write in straight lines in an empty box. Put lined paper underneath the form so that the lines show through and act as a guide. Alternatively, you can pencil fine lines on to the form itself, as long as you remember to rub them out carefully before you send off the finished application. A black pen should always be used as blue ink does not show up well if the form is photocopied (for other people in the company). Make sure that the pen you use does not blotch and smudge on the paper by buying or borrowing a good quality ink pen.

Style

Writing the form out neatly is important, but so are ordering the contents logically and making the key points stand out. It is difficult to absorb information from the printed page and trying to conjure up a picture of an individual from answers on a form is even more problematic. Yet that is what the employer is trying to do when he or she reads your form. Therefore it makes sense to think through in some detail what you want to convey. The best answers are not written straight on to the page but considered and arranged before the act of writing them down.

Some applicants think that they should change their style of writing to make it more formal and try to use long and complicated words that they would not normally use. Far from impressing the reader, this can sound stilted and old fashioned, which is probably not the way that you want to appear. You can be confident that if you write as though you are talking directly to the reader, you will sound fine. The important thing to concentrate on, as far as style is concerned, is that your writing is easy to read and understand.

You cannot assume that the reader knows what you are talking about unless you have explained clearly and simply. You should aim to tread the fine line between giving enough detail and ensuring that you are concise in your explanations. You will see from the example on page 36 that the use of note form can help here.

Layout

Think about the layout of the writing on the page when you are filling in your first rough copy. Each piece of information should be enclosed in its own border of white space to keep it separate from the next item. The contents of your form can be made to look more attractive and eye-catching with the judicious use of underlining, so make your qualifications and job titles stand out from the rest of the information presented. The example on page 36 illustrates this and bullet points can also be used to show the key elements.

Additional sheets of paper

If the application form invites you to 'continue on a separate sheet of paper if necessary', it is best to do so. The employer is indicating that he or she thinks it likely that you will need more space than that provided to give an adequate answer. Most of the other applicants will be using the extra space allowed, so your answer will look brief in comparison if you do not do the same.

It makes sense to keep a supply of stationery if you are applying for jobs. Good quality envelopes and paper make a difference to the way your application looks and mean that you are never without the 'tools' to apply for any job that comes up.

Some common problems

'My writing is too big to fit into the spaces provided.'
The advantage in completing your form on a rough copy first is
that you can spend time arranging your answers to fit the form.
You must scale down your writing to ensure that you have room
to answer adequately, even if you need several attempts to get it
small enough.

'My experience doesn't seem to tally with what the job requires.'
It may be that the job is not suitable for you, in which case you
need to do more thinking about the sort of work you are looking
for. It is difficult to get a job when you have no relevant
qualifications, experience or attributes. If you are trying to break
into a new career you will need to prove that, although different,
your previous experience has given you the type of skills that will
enable you to make a contribution to the company concerned.

**'I have only just left college and don't have any work experience
yet.'**
The challenge here is to minimise your weakness – that you have
not yet worked – and maximise your experiences at college. It
need not be formal work experience that counts here. You could
offer experience of voluntary work or part-time jobs as substi-
tutes. Helping out in a local project can show that you have
commitment to a certain type of work and that you have picked
up the skills demanded in the job you are applying for.

**'I didn't do well at school and don't have any qualifications to
put down.'**
You need not worry about this as long as you have something
else to offer the employer. Your work experience can show that
you learn quickly, apply yourself and can take a disciplined
environment.

**'I just can't get excited about the job. I keep putting off the task
of filling in the form.'**
It may be necessary to consider whether this job is really the one

for you. If you have spent some time thinking about the form and how your skills, personality and experience are suitable for it, and yet still cannot work up any enthusiasm for the task, perhaps it is not worth bothering. Many application forms are thrown away without being completed because the applicants find the closing date has arrived and they have made no progress with the form.

We all find filling in application forms hard work, and this often makes the task seem daunting. Most people underestimate the time needed to do the job properly. It may be that you need to devote more time and energy to the task. You really have to summon up all your confidence and pride in order to sell yourself to the employer and be ready to take at least as many days as there are pages in the form to do it justice.

'Some of my answers only fill in a few lines when the space provided is huge.'

This probably means that you have not spent enough time preparing your answers. The space given usually corresponds to the size of the answer that you are expected to give. Imagine your form being considered along with the others. If yours obviously has shorter answers, it may be rejected without being read.

'Even making my writing as small as possible, I need more space than that provided on the form.'

It may be that you started filling in the form without doing a rough copy first in order to work out the spacing required. If the form you are completing is really inadequate for the answers you think are required, you may have to use a separate sheet of paper but do make sure that you are not being long-winded in your answers. You should try to make your replies as concise and simple as possible otherwise you may lose your reader's attention.

'I have filled in all my personal details on the form but cannot complete the question about my personality strengths. It's too hard.'

This is one of the most important questions on the form. Employers may well appoint a candidate on the basis of his or her personality who does not have all the desired experience. You need to spend more time thinking about yourself and the sort of person the organisation is looking for. Use the exercise on page 19 to give you some help and rack your brains to collect all the ideas you can about the sort of person you are. Ask friends and relatives for suggestions – but remind them that you only want to hear *good* comments!

'I have finished the rough copy of my form but I am nervous that it may still have mistakes in it, even after I've checked it through.'
It is possible to spend so long poring over the document that it becomes impossible to see how well you have done. Have a rest from it for a while and do something totally different. Then come back to the task. Imagine that you have never seen the document before. Does it look well laid out and inviting to a reader? Is your writing tidy and neatly displayed? Are the main points of the form highlighted clearly but unfussily? Show the draft to friends and ask them to check it, and invite their comments on the way you have completed the answers and the way the form looks as a whole.

CHAPTER 5
Guidelines and Examples

Keeping records

When you have applied for a job, keep a copy of the application that you have sent off. You can file it along with the original advert and any paperwork sent to you by the company about the job. A ring-binder or wallet-style folder is ideal for this. Date your application form so that you know when you sent it off. Some employers inform you on the job details that unsuccessful applicants will not be notified, but otherwise they should let you know the outcome.

Follow-up

If you do not hear from the employer and you are expecting a reply, you can always ring up to find out what has happened to your application. Make sure that you allow a realistic period for the employer to process the applications and always be polite and courteous when you call.

'I applied for that factory job. Why haven't I heard from you yet?'

This sounds aggressive and is likely to antagonise whoever picks up the telephone. A better approach would be:

'I wonder if you can help me. I recently sent in an application to work in your company and would like to ask if there is any news about an interview shortlist yet.'

Employers and managers know that applicants are eager to get an interview and will try to be helpful if you sound pleasant and friendly. Similarly, if you are not offered an interview, you could contact the company to try to get some hints about why you were unsuccessful. This depends on your nerve, but a suggested formula could be:

'Thank you for informing me that I have not been successful in my job application. Would it be possible for someone to give me some brief ideas about improving my approach to future vacancies? I would be very grateful for any help that you can offer.'

Examples

The following examples show different questions frequently asked on application forms and explain how you should approach your answers.

Please describe your main non-work or non-academic interests and tell us why these give you particular satisfaction.
This question is asking about your hobbies and interests but it will not be enough to give a list here. You will need to say why you pursue these interests and what you do with your time. For instance:

'I am a member of the Northern Cycling Club and regularly participate in group rides. I believe that non-motorised transport is beneficial for the environment and I act as publicity officer for the Club to encourage more cycle-ways in cities and attract more members.'

'I have played and watched football for the last twenty years. I attend my local team's matches whenever possible and coach local youngsters in the season. It is satisfying to help foster talent in other people in this way.'

'I have a talent for baking cakes and make elaborate ones for friends and family when there is a special occasion. I won a prize for an Easter cake last year and was featured in the local paper as a result.'

'I read modern novels as a way of relaxing after work. I have recently tried to do some writing myself and joined a creative writing course to learn the right way to approach the subject.'

What has been your greatest achievement to date?

You must choose what to answer for yourself here, but think why the employer is asking this question. He or she will make a judgement not so much about the example you give, but why you think of it as an achievement.

Some ways of answering could include:

'Bringing up my family has to be my greatest achievement. I am proud of the fact that I have good relationships with all three children now they are older and I always make it my first priority to keep a good atmosphere.'

This tells the employer that the candidate is likely to be a helpful person to have around the office – someone who can perhaps stop team conflict before it arises.

'At school I studied a vocational course in the sixth form. Part of the course involved a study of a local factory and I found that I learnt a lot. At the end of the work I had to give a presentation to the whole year group. Despite feeling sick with nerves before I went on, I did my best and now will not feel so shy if I have to talk to a big group again. I learnt that doing plenty of preparation helps you to feel more confident about managing the task.'

This indicates a completely different approach from a younger applicant, and shows that the candidate was determined and quick to learn from the experience.

Please give your reasons for applying for this post.

The way that you answer this question depends on the sort of position applied for but here is an example:

'I am applying for this post because I am a skilled technician and believe that I have a lot to contribute to the job. In my present job I work closely with the pharmacist on duty and make sure that the supplies of drugs and medicines are clearly and safely displayed. I am a hard-working member of the team and can cope with an uneven pressure of work. I communicate well with my superiors and colleagues at all times. I enjoy this work very much and would relish the opportunity to contribute to the work of the General Hospital.'

What do you think you would like/dislike most about this job?
When answering this type of question be careful that you do not labour on about the problems to be encountered. Employers want to know that potential candidates are keen and enthusiastic, so a long list of how enjoyable you would find the work will help here.

Is there anything about your health record that you feel we should know?
This type of question is often asked when good health is a requirement of the job. You must use your common sense about the extent to which you reveal your medical history, but if any past illnesses are completely recovered from or would have no effect on your ability to do the job, they should not be mentioned. Be aware that if you do discuss some medical problem on the form, the employer will take it into account when considering your application, so the onus is on you to reassure him or her that you could do the job perfectly well, if this is the case.

Any question relating to time not accounted for, including employment.
This type of question is looking for evidence that you have spent your time profitably. Even if you have been out of work for a long spell, you should be able to show that you have picked up new skills, or perhaps travelled or done some voluntary work while looking for a job.

Here is an example of a completed application form for a local authority position. It shows the different sections which nor-mally appear.

From the information given so far, you will see that there are some important basic rules to follow when making applications.

APPLICATION FORM	Thank you for your interest - the following information is necessary to ensure that full consideration can be given to all candidates. Whilst the information is confidential, it will be necessary for a small number of authorised staff to have access to it during the selection process. To make copying easier it would be helpful if you would use black ink or type your replies.
Job applied for	ADMINISTRATIVE OFFICER
Department	Social Services
Reference number	SS 238H
Closing date	5.2.92.
Please return this form to	Personnel Section, Social Services Department,

Where did you see the job advertised?

THE LONDON ECHO NEWSPAPER

Personal Details

1 Last name **BISHOP**
2 First names **LESLEY**
3 Preferred title (eg. Mr, Mrs, Miss, Ms) **MISS**
4 Date of birth **4-9-60**
5 Home address **59 LITTLEACRE ROW**
LONDON
E14 9TN

Telephone   Home **071-000-0000**
Please include the code.
Office **071-000-0000**

May we contact you at work?   Yes ☑ No ☐

6 Employment Record (present or most recent employer first)

Employer's name and address	Job title and main duties	Dates employed and reason for leaving	Salary /Benefits/ Grade where appropriate (Proof may be required)
BAILEY'S GENERAL STORE HIGH STREET LONDON E14	ADMINISTRATOR : LOOKING AFTER ALL THE PAPERWORK AND WAGES FOR STAFF, DEALING WITH ACCOUNTS ENQUIRIES BY LETTER AND TELE-PHONE, FILING AND WRITING LETTERS, PAYING INVOICES	AUGUST 1985 TO DATE I WOULD LIKE TO WORK IN A LARGER ORGANISATION	£10,000 PH.
STEADFAST INSURANCE COMPANY MAIN ROAD SIDCUP, KENT	ADMINISTRATIVE ASSISTANT : HELPING OUT IN THE OFFICE, FILING AND SORTING DOCUMENTS, PROCESSING CLAIMS, ANSWERING THE TELEPHONE ENQUIRIES DUTY, ARRANGING MEETINGS AND TAKING AND TYING MINUTES	APRIL 1981 TO AUGUST 1985 I WAS OFFERED A MORE RESPONSIBLE JOB ELSEWHERE	£8,000 p.a.
BERYL'S FASHION STORE, THE PARADE, LONDON E1	SALES ASSISTANT: HELPING CUSTOMERS, ORDERING STOCK FROM HEAD OFFICE, KEEPING SHOP CLEAN AND TIDY, WINDOW DISPLAY, CASHING-UP TILL AND HANDLING MONEY, BANKING TAKINGS EACH DAY, PAPERWORK.	1978 TO MARCH 1981	£7,000 pa.

7 Please give details of any voluntary or community work you have been involved with or any outside activities relevant to the post applied for.

I LIKE HELPING OTHER PEOPLE AND DO SHOPPING FOR ELDERLY PEOPLE ON MY ESTATE. THEY ALSO OFTEN ASK ME TO SEE TO THEIR PAPERWORK AND BILLS FOR THEM. I ENJOY HELPING THEM TO KEEP THEIR AFFAIRS IN ORDER.
I ALSO HELP TO RAISE MONEY EACH YEAR FOR A LOCAL HOSPICE. I ORGANISE FUNDRAISING EVENTS WITH A COMMITTEE OF PEOPLE AND TAKE PART MYSELF IN THE DIFFERENT ACTIVITIES. LAST YEAR WE RAISED £5,500 FOR NEW EQUIPMENT.

8 Secondary and Higher Education / Courses attended

	Examinations passed and professional qualifications obtained with grades and dates including current studies if any.	
Dates		Grades
1972 - 1977	HILLTOPS SECONDARY SCHOOL, WANSTEAD ROAD LONDON SE16. O' LEVELS IN ENGLISH AND BIOLOGY CSE IN MATHS AND HOME ECONOMICS	C, C 1, 2
1981 - 1983	EVENING CLASSES IN BASIC BOOKKEEPING AT SIDCUP ADULT EDVCATION INSTITUTE, LONGSTREET SIDCUP.	PASSED ALL EXAMS

9 The Council wishes to encourage people with disabilities to apply for jobs - all information will be treated in confidence.

(i) Do you have a disability?   Yes ☐ No ☑

(ii) If yes, are you currently registered as disabled?   Yes ☐ No ☐

What is the nature of your disability?

N/A

(iii) Do you require special facilities or assistance at the interview or with any aspects of the job if appointed?   Yes ☐ No ☑
If yes please give details on a separate sheet.

10 If you are applying for job sharing do you have a job share partner?   Yes ☐ No ☐
If yes, please give their name and address.

N/A

11 Do you require a work permit?   Yes ☐ No ☑

12 Notice required by present employer _____ONE MONTH_____

13 Are there any dates when you will not be available for interview?
No

14 Do you hold a full current driving licence?   Yes ☑ No ☐

15 Are you related to any Councillor or senior officer of the Council?   Yes ☐ No ☑
If yes give details

Warning - Canvassing of or failing to disclose relationship to a Councillor may disqualify the candidate.

16 Those invited for interview may be required to answer formal questions as to whether or not they have unspent convictions or criminal charges or summonses pending against them. Certain posts, eg in Social Services or the Education Department, are exempt from the provisions of the Rehabilitation of Offenders Act 1974. Some posts are subject to political restrictions. If any of the above apply to the post you are applying for, further details will be made available to you.

17 Please add below details of any special skills, experience or qualifications which make you particularly suited for this job. (An additional sheet may be added if necessary.)

> I ENJOYED SUBJECTS AT SCHOOL WHICH INVOLVED WRITTEN WORK AND WHEN I GOT MY FIRST OFFICE JOB, I WENT TO NIGHT-SCHOOL TO STUDY BOOK-KEEPING. I TOOK TO THIS SUBJECT QUICKLY AND PASSED MY EXAMS, COMING TOP OF THE YEAR GROUP FOR DOUBLE-ENTRY WORK. AT THE INSURANCE COMPANY I LEARNT HOW TO KEEP A BUSY OFFICE WORKING SMOOTHLY AND I FOUND HELPING TO SORT OUT CLIENTS' PROBLEMS WAS VERY SATISFYING. I WAS ASKED TO RUN THE ACCOUNTS OFFICE AT BAILEY'S STORE AND TOOK RESPONSIBILITY FOR ALL THE FINANCIAL DEALINGS OF THIS COMPANY. I AM A MATURE, CALM INDIVIDUAL WHO RESPECTS OTHER PEOPLE AND CAN HELP TO GET THE BEST FROM A STAFF TEAM. I WORK WELL UNDER PRESSURE AND ALWAYS KEEP TO DEADLINES. I HAVE HIGH STANDARDS AND PREFER TO WORK IN A SMALL TEAM OF COLLEAGUES. I AM AN ACCURATE TYPIST, AND CAN BE RELIED UPON TO TAKE RESPONSIBILITY WHEN THE OCCASION ARISES. I AM ESSENTIALLY OF A HAPPY DISPOSITION AND ENJOY BEING FULLY OCCUPIED AT WORK

18 Please give the name and address of two referees (other than relatives), both of whom should if possible be previous employers, including your present or most recent employer. If school/college leaver please give the name and address of head teacher/tutor. Internal applicants should give the name and extension of their section head.

i) MR MATTHEW BELTON
69 UNDERDOWN LANE
FROGHAMPTON
HAMPSHIRE
SO42 1TT

ii) MRS JUNE BAILEY (OWNER)
% BAILEY'S GENERAL STORE
HIGH STREET
LONDON
E14 7TT.

If shortlisted, references may be taken up prior to interview. If you do not want us to approach your present employer at this stage please tick box. ☑

If you were known by another name when employed please specify: ___—___

19 I declare that the particulars set out in this application are true in all respects.

Signed _Lesley Bishop_   Date _27 - 7 - 92_

52

Dos

Do allow yourself plenty of time to complete the form. A rushed application may lose you the job and copies sent by facsimile machine never create such a good impression.

Do write out your application in rough first. The more care you take over the task, the better your chances of success.

Do read the form through carefully first and then follow all the instructions. Plan your answers before you write anything.

Do stress your good points. Let the employer know that he or she would be lucky to have you as an employee.

Do make clear and concise points when you write. Waffle is not impressive but personal examples to back up your claims will do the trick.

Don'ts

Don't send in your form after the closing date. It is unlikely to be considered unless you have gained the employer's permission in advance.

Don't scribble out mistakes. Use correction fluid or put one neat line through the material concerned using a ruler.

Don't send in your CV with an application form unless you are asked to do so.

Don't miss out any questions. Check the completed form thoroughly before you send it off. Boxes left blank can give an impression of off-handedness.

Don't tell lies. You could lose your job if you are found out.

CHAPTER 6
Letters of Application

Some job advertisements ask you to send in your CV (curriculum vitae) together with a letter of application. Read *Preparing Your Own CV* (see page 87) to find out how to put together a CV of which you can be proud. Sending a CV to a company with no letter of explanation is confusing, so you need to write a bold, confident and clear letter to accompany it. The letter should be addressed to the named person if you are replying to an advertisement, and it is often helpful to say where you saw the vacancy advertised.

If you are sending the letter as a speculative approach, just to see if the organisation has any vacancies, try to find out the name of the right person to contact and address the letter to him or her personally.

The letter needs to explain the following:

● why you are sending your CV
● significant things about your background and skills
● the sort of person you are
● what you would like to happen next
● how you can be contacted.

Everyone who applies for jobs in this way sends in a dynamic letter with their CV, so yours must be strong in order to compete. The letter cannot just be a brief note to say why the CV has arrived; it must be the selling point of the application. Do not make it longer than two sides, and the tone should be courteous and detailed. Do not worry about repeating information contained in your CV. The letter may well be separated from the CV and, in any case, it does no harm to re-state your good points.

You should use good quality paper and word-processed or typed documents are now the norm rather than hand-writing. However neat your writing, it is not the same as the employer's and is therefore not nearly as easy to read as typed script. Prove this for yourself by seeing how much faster it is to read newsprint than a letter from someone you do not know.

Examples

The following pages contain five examples of letters of application for people in different situations. One or more of them may be relevant to you, as you consider how to compose your own letters to employers.

These examples are included to give you an idea of the many different ways in which such letters can be written. Although the names and addresses are fictitious, all the details come from letters written by successful job-seekers. No letter will be appropriate for every situation, but the examples have been chosen to represent a range of circumstances. Do not copy these letters, but see if they give you ideas for approaches of your own.

1 Speculative approach

Maria MacDonald
Basement Flat
2 Arbour Fields
Richmond
N Yorks

15 April 1993

Mr David Belton
Director
Salcott Equipment
33 Pinks Lane
Richmond
N Yorks

Dear Mr Belton

I am writing to enquire if you have any vacancies in your company. I enclose my CV for your information. As you can see, I have spent ten years working with a variety of different machinery and equipment and am used to industrial work.

I am a steady and serious person who works hard and fits easily into a new team. I am clean and careful in my work and can lend a hand in the office when needed. I am quick to pick up new instructions and flexible about the hours that I work. It was normal for me to do shift-work in my last job. I am known for taking a pride in my work and want to work for a company with a reputation for producing quality goods – hence my application to Salcott's.

I have excellent references and would be delighted to discuss any possible vacancy with you at your convenience. In case you do not have any suitable openings at the moment, I would be grateful if you would keep my CV on file for any future possibilities.

Thank you for your attention to this matter. I look forward to hearing from you.

Yours sincerely

Maria MacDonald

Enc:

2 College leaver

Adrian Miller
97 Potter's Close
Sedgefield
Teesside
RT3 3PP

25 October 1992

Ms Louise Powell
Powell's Energy Company
200 Seymour Industrial Estate
Hartfield Road
Middlesbrough GT99 1LZ

Dear Ms Powell

Please find enclosed my CV in application for the post advertised in the *Guardian* on 20 October.

The nature of my degree course has prepared me for this position. The course involved a great deal of independent research, relying on a substantial amount of translating into French and Spanish. I also studied economic history and for one course (History of Latin America since Independence) an understanding of the petro-chemical industry was essential. I found this subject very stimulating.

I am a fast and accurate writer, with a keen eye for detail and I should be very grateful for the opportunity to progress to market reporting.

I have not only the ability to take on the responsibility of this position immediately, but I believe that I also have the enthusiasm and determination to ensure that I make a success of it.

Thank you for taking the time to consider this application and I look forward to hearing from you in the near future.

Yours sincerely

Adrian Miller

Enc:

3 Woman returner

Sherena Williams
Hazelwood Cottage
Sandy Hill
Sway
Hampshire

13 December 1992

The Personnel Manager
Hall's Ltd
100 London Road
Brockenhurst
Hampshire

Dear Sir/Madam

Re: Accounts Manager Vacancy

I am writing in reply to your advertisement in this week's *Hampshire Times*. I enclose my CV for your information. As you can see, I trained in accounting at Bishop's Technical College gaining a BTEC pass in 1982. For the next four years I ran the accounts department of Nicholson's Bakery in Lymington. I covered the whole variety of work in this busy office, from handling petty cash and making wage payments to credit control.

I left this post in 1986 to bring up my two young children. Being a full-time parent has enabled me to acquire new skills, such as scheduling and keeping to deadlines, organising, communicating on different levels, delegating work and using my creative imagination to solve problems.

I am patient and flexible, stay calm in difficult situations, and am confident when working with figures and running an office. I am hard-working and thorough and am looking forward to resuming my career with a pace-making organisation like Hall's.

I would be happy to discuss this application in more detail and look forward to hearing from you.

Yours faithfully

Sherena Williams

Enc:

4 School/College leaver

Fola Okintola
111 Poulton Terrace
Sidcup
Kent

1 September 1992

The Personnel Director
Haddleston Council
Haddleston
Kent

Dear Sir/Madam

Re: Vacancies for Junior Trainees

I would like to apply for the vacancy for junior trainee which I saw in my local careers office.

I left Cole Comprehensive School this year after taking my GCSE exams. I passed in English, Mathematics and General Science and won a prize for a project on 'Science and Ecology' earlier in my final year. I enclose a copy of my CV and my Record of Achievement which shows my progress throughout the last two years.

I am good at bringing the best out of other people and spent my sports lessons at school being a key player in the volleyball team. I have worked each summer for the last three years as an assistant in the local sports centre helping to organise the summer sports programme which the Council runs each year for school children.

I am interested in working for the Council because I believe that local services are important. I take a pride in living in this area and know that your recent Quality Initiative has made people realise how much they depend on good street lighting and cleaning, housing and leisure facilities.

I would like to become a part of the team of people who organise such services and look forward to discussing how I can contribute to the work of the Council in due course.

Thank you for your time. I look forward to hearing from you.

Yours faithfully

Fola Okintola

Enc:

5 Mature candidate

Louis Coombe
80 Bryan Ridge
Westminster Parade
London SW15

15 February 1993

Mrs Alberga
Personnel Manager
Kogan and Company
Norman Street
London W1

Dear Mrs Alberga

Re: Adviser, Training Unit

Please find enclosed my CV. I have had many years' successful experience as a personnel manager in the clothing industry. Working with teams of different people meant that I quickly became adaptable and flexible.

I am at present updating my computer skills at a local resource centre and I have been helping the tutors there, on a voluntary basis, with the new trainees. I introduce them to the centre and act as a mentor during their training programme.

I devote time to making sure that everyone works well together and can recognise problems before they become insurmountable. I am approachable and tolerant but maintain high standards and the ability to communicate quickly and clearly with others. I am known for my ability to make learning fun and can always motivate people to give more of themselves. My mature outlook allows me to be a soothing influence at difficult times and I have a wide experience of work to draw on when needed.

I would enjoy contributing to the training provided by your company as I know of your excellent reputation in this field. I have a relative who works in your Northern Region who tells me that your staff development programme is very good.

I would be delighted to discuss any detail of my application at your convenience. Thank you for your attention to this matter. I look forward to hearing from you.

Yours sincerely

Louis Coombe

Enc:

Notice how in each of these examples the candidates are trying to phrase their application in terms that will appeal to the employer. They have thought through:

- what the job involves
- what they have to offer in skills and experience
- how their personalities will fit.

They have made sure that they convey this clearly and simply in their letters. They sound keen without giving the impression that they are desperate. Most important, they spend time demonstrating to the reader how they can contribute to the organisation.

Notice also how they write the letter itself. They know that their letter must be easy to read and follow if they are to attract the employer's attention when he or she has a pile of other applications to consider. They write as if they were sitting in front of the employer at an interview – clearly but politely. Good writing does not mean using the longest words and the most complicated sentences that you can think up. It means being concise and to the point, and keeping your sentences short.

None of the letters is gimmicky or flashy. All the writers believe that they have serious skills to offer and the right personalities to fit into the environment concerned. Their letters convey that information to the employer in an impressive way. You can tell that each writer has spent time and trouble composing the letter in order to make sure that it hits the mark.

Each letter ends with a thank you and is correctly addressed and typed for easy reading.

CHAPTER 7
How to Get That Job!

Step-by-step checklist

Step 1. Planning

When you receive your application form take a copy and put the original away safely until you are ready to write up the final version. Now read your copy through carefully. Re-read the job advertisement and any other details of the job or company that you may have, including the job description and personnel specification. These documents will tell you exactly how the employer will rate you for your suitability for the position. You may wish to do some other research into the business or the type of work involved.

A *job description*, as its name suggests, describes the main activities in the job. It lists, often in order of importance, the work that the successful candidate will be doing. You need to use this document to show how you could cope with the job. Do not just state that you are capable of everything that is asked for, but rather give brief examples to illustrate what you have achieved in these areas previously.

A *personnel specification* is a list prepared by employers in relation to a particular job, to describe the type of person that they are looking for. It details the character traits that they would like and those particular skills or experience that may be ESSENTIAL or PREFERRED for the post.

If a personnel specification is included with the details sent to you about a job, it is not there just for guidance in filling out the form. You *must* show that you possess any ESSENTIAL skills or qualities asked for. Your application will be more favourably considered if you can also demonstrate that you have those PREFERRED for the work. A simple assertion that you have the skill required will not do. You need to take each requirement in turn and think of an example which shows your ability in this area.

Spend time thinking about the sort of person you are, recap your employment history, mulling over the things that you have done particularly well in the past, and any praise that you received in the work environment or in a personal capacity. Take stock of your CV and think of work-related examples which will prove to an employer that you would be good at the job advertised. Boost your confidence as much as possible so that you will not hold back once you start filling in your application. Most candidates fail at this stage because they do not present their good points and strengths adequately.

Step 2. Preparation

Now you are ready to do some serious work to tie up what the employer is looking for with your experience. Spend some time thinking over the details of the job. You can use your common sense to work out what sort of person the employer is looking for. Does he or she need any specific skills or experience? Underline all the key points from the original advertisement, job description and personnel specification.

Remember that you can describe the same job in different ways. For example, in one case you may emphasise the experience you gained in handling projects and achieving targets through communicating with people. In another case you may need to emphasise the amount of work you did, analysing and interpreting data, preparing reports and contributing to the development of new ideas, policies and procedures. Draft your answers on your copy and make sure that you respond to all the questions and fill up all the available space. It has been provided for that purpose and half-empty boxes will not be sufficient.

Remember that the employer is also interested in your personality. Make sure that you analyse your strengths and personal characteristics so that you can demonstrate your suitability for the job. Job applicants tend to spend a great deal of time writing about their skills and experience and expend too little effort in trying to convey their character traits, when the latter may be the most important factor to the employer.

Think back through your work experience, whether paid or voluntary, and choose examples which tie in with the work involved in this job to show how you would be a good employee. Put your answers down on the page. You may need to make two or three attempts before you feel happy with your answer, particularly with the difficult questions such as: 'What skills and experience do you have that make you particularly suitable for this job?' These questions are meant to test you, to see if you can provide a well thought-out and appropriate answer, so take them seriously.

Take plenty of time at this stage. As a general rule, the number of days that you work on this form from start to finish should equal the number of pages of the form.

Get a friend or relative to check over the rough copy of the form for you. They may spot missed questions or spelling mistakes that you have not noticed, and can see if your answers make sense.

Step 3. Putting it all together

Once you are satisfied with your answers, you can transfer your work on to the final copy of the form. Take great care – this must be as neat as you can possibly make it. You will be judged mainly on the way that you present yourself on paper, and no matter how excellent your answers, if the form looks messy you are unlikely to be chosen for interview. Take pride in the application and enjoy the challenge of showing off your attributes and talents. Again, at this stage, get someone to look at the form for you. Silly mistakes are easy to miss when you have been buried in the same form for ages. Have you remembered to sign it at the bottom if asked to do so? Keep a copy of the finished version that you send off, and put the date on it, so that you have a neat record of what the employer will see.

Step 4. Follow-up

You need to be systematic about your job-hunting. When you send off your completed form, keep a copy for your records (just in case you are called for interview) and store the copy together with the original advert and any other information that you may have about the job. Perhaps all these pieces of paper could be put in a special file, dated, and kept tidily in case you need to refer to them again. You may apply for a similar job in the future, and you can save yourself some work if you have already thought out your answers.

Unless the employer has told you that you will only be notified if you are shortlisted for the vacancy, you should expect to hear from the company after the closing date. It does not hurt to get in touch with the employer if you are not contacted. A friendly enquiry (something like: 'I applied for a vacancy with your company recently but have not heard from you yet. I wonder if I could ask if there is any news.') may answer your question. Remember not to sound aggressive on the telephone. 'I applied for a job with you two weeks ago. Why haven't you called me for interview?' will probably not encourage a positive reply.

The point of following up vacancies in this way is twofold. First, there is always the possibility that your application may have been mislaid or forgotten and your call may help to sort out the problem. Second, even if you have not been successful you could ask the employer for tips to help you improve future attempts.

Handling rejection is not easy for any of us and yet we all need to be able to keep moving forward. Resist the inclination to think that there is something wrong with you if you are turned down for a job. If you genuinely feel that you worked hard on your application and represented your experience, skills and personality as best you could, you should congratulate yourself. If the employer had the chance to get to know you through your form, perhaps you were not quite suitable for the vacancy compared to other candidates. The reason why you did not succeed can only be guessed at, but it is likely that there just happened to be someone with more appropriate experience than you on the day.

Your turn will soon come as long as you keep your standards

of presentation as high as possible. The chances are that there is an even better job just round the corner. You can take comfort from the fact that all the work you put in on your application may come in useful for a similar vacancy in the future, with some minor alterations to gear it up to the next job.

The best antidote to feeling demoralised is to keep on applying for other jobs. If possible, each time you are waiting to hear about one job, send off an application for another so that you always have one to look forward to. Sometimes it is a disheartening experience to feel that you are not succeeding with your job search. You need to keep your confidence high by feeling a sense of achievement in some other area of your life. Participate in some voluntary work, where your abilities will be appreciated while you wait to get a job, or learn a new skill to improve your chances of being shortlisted for interview.

Above all, keep believing that you are special, that you have a lot to offer and that you will eventually arrive at where you want to be. As soon as you are in a satisfying job, this period of making applications, which seems to be dragging on, will be hard to recall. If you are reading this book without any particular job to apply for at the moment, remember to re-read it when you have your next important form to complete. Good luck!

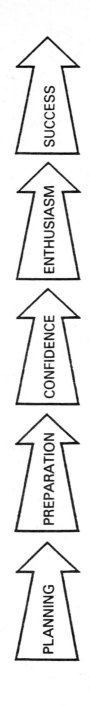

Application form blanks

You may find these blank forms useful to practise on, even if there is no particular job vacancy that you are interested in at the moment. Use the checklist on pages 63–7 to remind you of the best way to complete them.

APPLICATION FORM
EDUCATION

Academic Qualifications (please give subjects)	Professional Qualifications (please give dates)

TRAINING COURSES

Organising Body	Title of Course	Dates Attended

Are you a car owner?   Yes/No
Do you hold a valid driving licence?   Yes/No

EMPLOYMENT HISTORY

Employer (current or most recent first)	Job title and brief description of duties	Grade	Salary	Dates employed	Reason for leaving

ADDITIONAL INFORMATION

Please give the following information:

(A) The reasons why you are applying for this post.
(B) Any experience you may have which is related to this post.

INTERESTS AND ACTIVITIES

Briefly outline your hobbies and interests

Please give the names and addresses of two referees:-
(ONE MUST BE YOUR PRESENT EMPLOYER)

NAME ....

POSITION ....

ADDRESS ....

....

....

....

POSTCODE ....

MAY WE CONTACT PRIOR TO
INTERVIEW?

YES/NO

NAME ....

POSITION ....

ADRESS ....

....

....

....

POSTCODE ....

MAY WE CONTACT PRIOR TO
INTERVIEW?

YES/NO

NOTICE PERIOD REQUIRED?

IF SELECTED FOR INTERVIEW WOULD YOU BE AVAILABLE ON

....? YES/NO

I confirm that to the best of my knowledge the information given on this form is
true and can be treated as any subsequent Contract of Employment.

Date .... Signature ....

APPLICATION FORM

For Office Use

APPLICATION FOR THE POST OF _____

PERSONAL DETAILS

FORENAME(S) _____ SURNAME _____

ADDRESS _____

_____

(INCLUDING POST CODE) _____

DATE OF BIRTH _____ SEX: MALE/FEMALE

TELEPHONE: HOME _____ DAYTIME _____

CURRENT DRIVING LICENCE: YES/NO CAR OWNER: YES/NO

Do you have any special requirements to enable you to attend for interview, eg access, interpreters? Please indicate below.

DETAILS OF EDUCATION, TRAINING AND QUALIFICATIONS

Dates Attended	Full-time or Part-time	Name and Town of Secondary School/College/ University	Qualifications/ Examinations – state subjects & examining board	Date Gained

REFERENCES

Two persons to whom approach may be made should be listed. If you do not wish any reference to be sought at this stage, please place an X in the relevant box.

Name: Name:

[ ] Full Address: [ ] Full Address:

Telephone No: Telephone No:

PLEASE INDICATE YOUR REASONS FOR SEEKING THIS POST,
HIGHLIGHTING ANY PERSONAL SKILLS WHICH YOU BELIEVE
WOULD BE OF PARTICULAR RELEVANCE OR VALUE.

PAST EMPLOYMENT   (Please include part-time or holiday jobs)

Employer: Type of Work/Responsibilities

VOLUNTARY WORK EXPERIENCE   (For example, involvement in
community fundraising, play group,
committee work.)

PRESENT EMPLOYMENT   (if applicable)

Employer's Name   ....

and Address   ....

                        ....

Date Started   ....

Type of Work/Responsibilities:

Confidential application form

Position applied for

How did you hear of the vacancy?

Surname (Mr/Mrs/Ms/Miss)

(BLOCK LETTERS PLEASE)

Address

Forenames

Telephone No. (Home)   (Work)

Nationality   Date of birth

Are you prepared to move house –

What locations in England and Wales would be most and least acceptable to you?

For this position   Most acceptable

For future promotion   Least acceptable

Do you have a full driving licence?   YES/NO

To assist us in monitoring our policy of equal opportunities, we would be grateful if you could tick the appropriate box.

I would describe my ethnic origin as

African	Afro-Caribbean	Asian	European-UK	European-other	Other – please specify
☐	☐	☐	☐	☐	☐

School Record (after age 11)

Name & address of School/College	Dates From	To	Educational Qualifications (specify all subjects and attempts)					
			'O' levels or equivalent					
			Subject	Grade	Date	Subject	Grade	Date
			'A' levels or equivalent					
			Subject	Grade	Date	Subject	Grade	Date

Further Education Record

Name of Universities/Colleges attended (f/t or p/t) plus dates	Subjects taken	BSc, BA etc	Qualification Level/Class expected or obtained	Date obtained

Professional Qualifications

Give the dates and results of all professional examinations taken (including intermediate stages)	Result	Dates

Employment History

Please give details of your present or most recent job

From   Main duties and responsibilities

To

Name and address of employer

                                              Main achievements

Nature of business

Job title   Organisation chart indicating your main position

Starting salary

Most recent salary

Reason for leaving

Please give details of your second most recent job

From   Main duties and responsibilities

To

Name and address of employer

                                              Main achievements

Nature of business

Job title   Organisation chart indicating your main position

Starting salary

Most recent salary

Reason for leaving

Please list any job before those mentioned overleaf

From	To	Name of employer	Job title	Salary	
				Start	Finish

Interests/Responsibilities

What are your main interests/responsibilities outside work?

Career Plans

Describe briefly the development of your career to date, your plans for the future and the attraction of this job.

Are there any particular questions you would like to raise at interview?

Any further information you may care to give which may be relevant to your application.

Referees

Please give the name, address and position of two referees who can comment on your work performance. At least one of these should be connected with your present (or most recent) place of employment or study.

1.   2.

Position   Position

Please give the name, address and occupation of one referee unconnected with employment who has known you for at least three years to whom reference may be made.

Occupation

Have you been convicted of any criminal offences which are not yet "spent" under the Rehabilitation of Offenders Act 1974?
(Please give details or answer 'No')

Please give details of any major illness and/or any chronic conditions/allergies.

Please give details of any time lost from work/full-time education in the last five years through ill health or other incapacity.

Are you registered disabled?   YES/NO

How much notice are you required to give?

Signature   **Date**

Note: a) It will be accepted that we may approach your past employers (BUT NOT YOUR PRESENT EMPLOYER), unless you make a note to the contrary below, showing the organisation we may not approach without prior permission.
b) Any false or misleading statements made on this form may, if they subsequently come to light, be taken to justify dismissal from employment with the Commission or could result in the cancellation of any job offer made.

Sources of Help

Careers offices

Careers officers work with young people and sometimes adults. They may be able to help you by checking over your form and they may provide access to a careers library where you can find information about different employers and jobs.

Libraries

Libraries can be a quiet place to complete application forms and the reference sections of main libraries have information about different companies and large employers so you can find out about the main products and services and the company organisation. Ask a librarian for help. Many libraries also have photocopiers for use by the public for a fee.

Job clubs

Government-funded job clubs have skilled staff who can advise you on the best way to make applications. If you have been unemployed for a while you can use their job search facilities such as telephones and stationery to help you get a job. Contact your local Jobcentre for details.

Further Reading from Kogan Page

Great Answers to Tough Interview Questions, 3rd edition, Martin John Yate

How to Pass Computer Selection Tests, Sanjay Modha

How to Pass Graduate Recruitment Tests, Mike Bryon

How to Pass Selection Tests, Mike Bryon and Sanjay Modha

How to Pass Technical Selection Tests, Mike Bryon and Sanjay Modha

How to Pass the Civil Service Qualifying Tests, Mike Bryon

How to Win as a Part-Time Student, Tom Bourner and Phil Race

The Jobhunter's Handbook, David Greenwood

Preparing Your Own CV, Rebecca Corfield

Successful Interview Skills, Rebecca Corfield

Test Your Own Aptitude, 2nd edition, Jim Barrett and Geoff Williams